Santa's
ANGELS

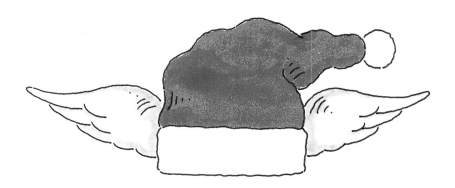

By Bonnie Altenhein

Illustrations by Monica Sheehan

Wings Books • New York • Avenel, New Jersey

This 1995 edition is published by Wings Books,
distributed by Random House Value Publishing, Inc.,
40 Engelhard Avenue, Avenel, New Jersey 07001,
by arrangement with the author.

Random House
New York • Toronto • London • Sydney • Auckland

Printed and bound in Mexico

Library of Congress Cataloging–in–Publication Data

Altenhein, Bonnie
Santa's angels / Bonnie Altenhein ; Monica Sheehan, illustrator.
p.   cm.
ISBN 0–517–14756–4 (Hardcover)
1. Christmas—United States 2. Angels. I. Title
GT4986.A1A45   1995   95–19382
394.2'663'0207—dc20   CIP

8 7 6 5 4 3 2 1

for gerry - b.a.

for gerry - monica

(life is just a bowl of gerry's)

Santa's angels are always on call, making merriment and miracles... sharing glad tidings of peace and goodwill. The holiday angel team is directly accountable to Santa 365 days a year — when you're sleeping or awake, acting naughty or nice — reporting casual acts of kindness, consideration and grace. Wherever there is holiday magic, Santa's angels are behind the scenes, busy orchestrating the wonder of Christmas and helping our dreams come true.

$\mathcal{R}$ejoice in the
wonder of Christmas.

Santa's angels cut out snowflakes from the clouds and paint the frost on your windows.

Hark when Santa's angels sing.

Santa's angels make sure everyone has something special for Christmas.

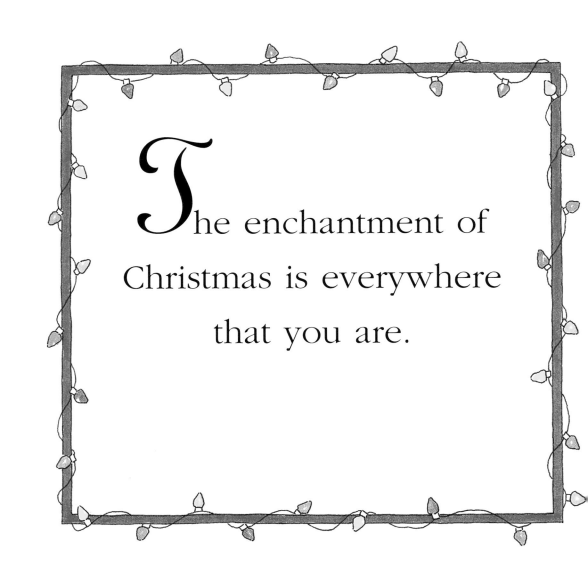

The enchantment of Christmas is everywhere that you are.

Santa's angels carry hope and joy to the world.

Christmas is not for conservative clothes.

Santa's angels work overtime so Santa can take a break with the elves.

$\mathcal{T}$he twelve days of
Christmas are easier
if you take them
one step at a time.

Santa's angels bring seasoned greetings to the kitchen.

*C*hristmas is for kids
from one to ninety-two.

Santa's angels never run out of wrapping paper.

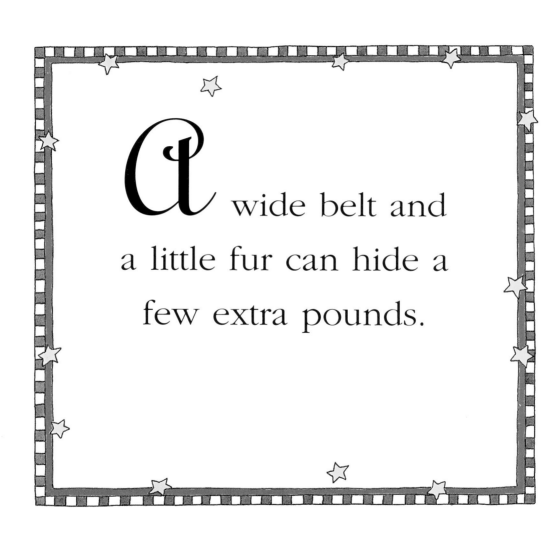

A wide belt and a little fur can hide a few extra pounds.

Santa's angels find a present for everyone on your shopping list.

$\mathcal{B}$uy yourself a Christmas present.

Santa's angels check his list twice.

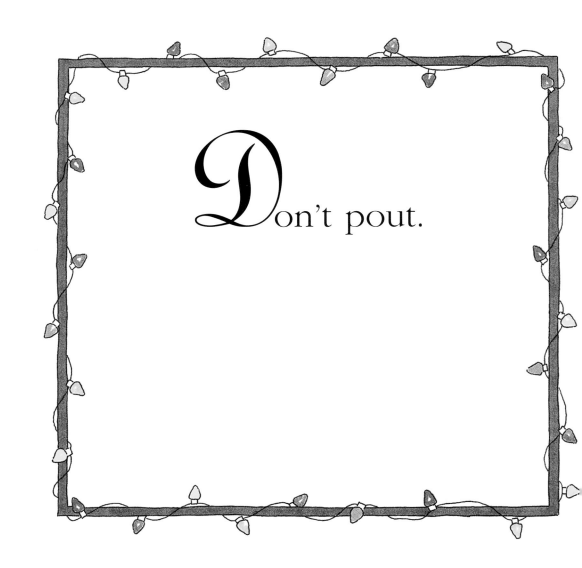

Don't pout.

Santa couldn't be everywhere, so he created angels.

Christmas is for believers.

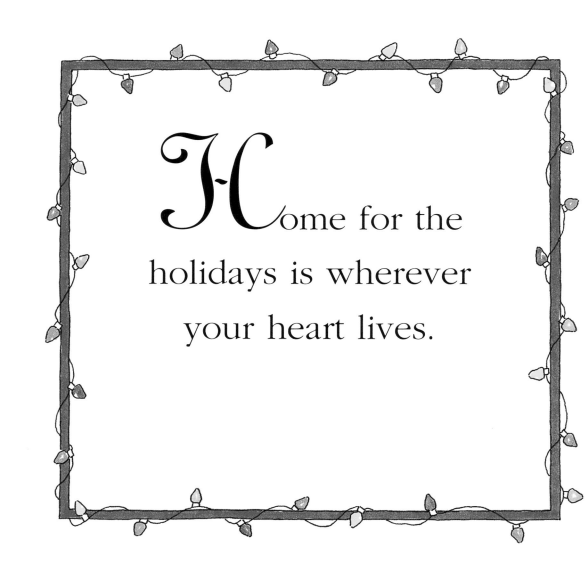

Home for the holidays is wherever your heart lives.

Don't get tangled up in the trivia of the season.

Share the spirit of Christmas with a friend.

Believing is seeing.

The miracle of Christmas is the wonder of you.

Santa's angels turn on the moon and light the stars so Santa can find his way.

Let there be a window to your heart so the light of the season shines through.

Wherever there is Christmas love, Santa's angels are behind the scenes.

Santa's angels help Santa down the chimney on Christmas eve.

Santa's angels are always on call.

Santa's angels make sure that batteries are included.

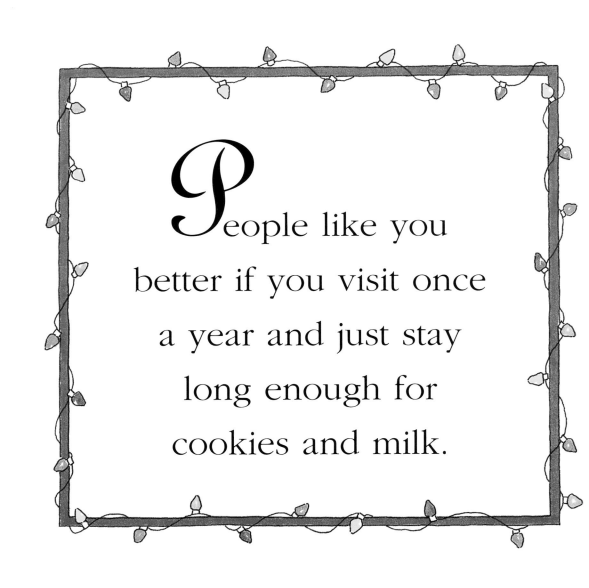

$\mathcal{P}$eople like you
better if you visit once
a year and just stay
long enough for
cookies and milk.

Santa's angels give gifts with no strings attached.

Santa's angels make
sure you receive only
one fruitcake per
holiday season.

Expect a Christmas miracle.

*I*t is kinder to give
than to receive.

Santa's angels dance
with Dancer.

Santa's angels know
the second verse of
"Jingle Bells."

$\mathcal{M}$emories are
made of Christmas.

Santa's angels can deliver the promise of peace on Earth.

Santa's angels believe in the possibilities of our Christmas dreams.

*C*hristmas is a
glorious new beginning.

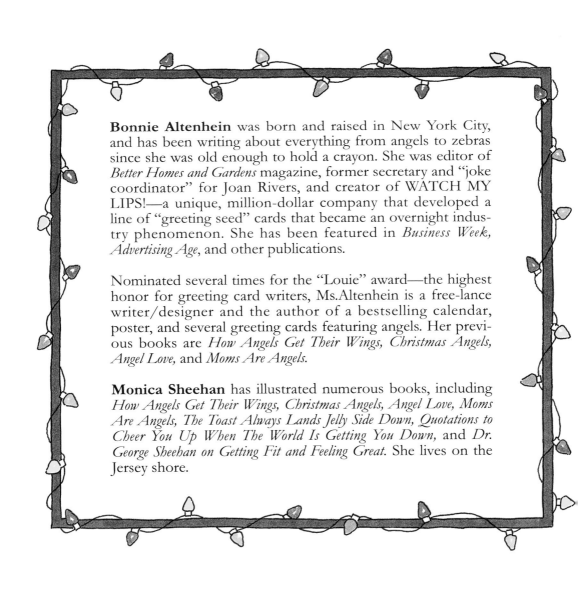

Bonnie Altenhein was born and raised in New York City, and has been writing about everything from angels to zebras since she was old enough to hold a crayon. She was editor of *Better Homes and Gardens* magazine, former secretary and "joke coordinator" for Joan Rivers, and creator of WATCH MY LIPS!—a unique, million-dollar company that developed a line of "greeting seed" cards that became an overnight industry phenomenon. She has been featured in *Business Week, Advertising Age*, and other publications.

Nominated several times for the "Louie" award—the highest honor for greeting card writers, Ms.Altenhein is a free-lance writer/designer and the author of a bestselling calendar, poster, and several greeting cards featuring angels. Her previous books are *How Angels Get Their Wings, Christmas Angels, Angel Love,* and *Moms Are Angels.*

Monica Sheehan has illustrated numerous books, including *How Angels Get Their Wings, Christmas Angels, Angel Love, Moms Are Angels, The Toast Always Lands Jelly Side Down, Quotations to Cheer You Up When The World Is Getting You Down,* and *Dr. George Sheehan on Getting Fit and Feeling Great.* She lives on the Jersey shore.